HIST in HURRY

Wild West

written and drawn by
JOHN FARMAN

MACMILLAN
CHILDREN'S BOOKS

CW00866326

All **HISTORY in a HURRY** *titles can be
ordered at your local bookshop or are available by post
from Book Service by Post (tel: 01624 675137).*

First published 1999 by Macmillan Children's Books
a division of Macmillan Publishers Limited
25 Eccleston Place, London SW1W 9NF
Basingstoke and Oxford

Associated companies throughout the world

ISBN 0 330 37647 0

Text and illustrations copyright © John Farman 1999

1 3 5 7 9 8 6 4 2

A CIP catalogue record for this book is available from the British Library.

Printed and bound in Great Britain by Mackays of Chatham plc, Kent

❧ CONTENTS

☁= *OFF WE GO!*

Ever since I was old enough to wear my first cowboy outfit (you should see the one I'm wearing now!), I've always been a real sucker for Westerns. Like most trainee gunslingers (I was Johnny the Kid), I never questioned the way the Wild West was portrayed in the movies. Brave, handsome wranglers trailing the wide open, inhospitable prairies in honest pursuit of their business (cows), and humble homesteaders (usually with dodgy foreign accents) who'd travelled from far-off places (like Birmingham) to settle and make their new home, America, a fit place for their adorable freckly children to grow up in. They were continually pestered by pesky Redskins,* who would appear from nowhere, whooping in a most vulgar manner, looting, murdering, pillaging and generally making an awful fuss. Either that or the poor old homesteaders would be robbed

* They have to be called Native Americans these days. Redskins, Indians, Red Indians, etc., just won't do. OK? *Ed*

(or worse) by all the baddie cowboys, who weren't really cowboys (or even boys) but seemed to like the clothes and shooting their guns off in public places.

The problem with the Wild West that we know and love is that most of the stories were just hyped up for the movies, and the truth is often much more difficult to find. But I sure am gonna try. That's if my editor lets me – she's responsible for those niggly little comments at the bottom of the pages. (She signs herself Ed., short for Editor.)

STOP PRESS

The original residents of the American Continent have now requested that they'd prefer to be called by their nation name (tribal, to you and me) – e.g. Sioux, Cheyenne, etc. – and that if we can't manage that, they'll make do with just 'Indian'.* Let's hope they don't change their minds again before I get to the end of this book . . .

* Redskin, however, is still Not On. Ed

Chapter 1

IN THE VERY BEGINNING (OR ... WHERE DID THOSE INDIANS COME FROM?)

When the first white men arrived in the New World (America) from the Old World (Europe), they came across strange high-cheekboned, deeply sun-tanned natives, who they later nick-named Red Indians. These were the first people ever to live in America and had had the place all to themselves for centuries.

Useless Fact No. 937
Red Indians weren't called that because of their skin colour, but because of the red warpaint they wore when going out.

But when did the Red Indians (as they no longer like to be called*) first show up? The most popular story goes like this. Way before the Stone Age, large numbers of wandering Mongolian nomads trudged across the Bering Straits (then a land bridge) from the freezing Russian and Siberian plains and set up home in what must have seemed a bit like Paradise. If all this ex-Russian business is true, I'm surprised the tribes weren't called names like the Cherokeesoviches or the Comanchniks. It is, however, important to note that from early on there were two main types of Indians – forest and prairie – and they both lived in very different ways.

* I've already explained that. Ed

Useless Fact No. 939

Apart from their not being Red, it seems that they weren't Indian either. They were only called Indian because old Christopher Columbus (see page 12) thought he'd arrived in India.

The history of the colonization of the American West (the vast plains that make up that big bit on the left of North America) is one of bravery, greed and tragedy, and a sometimes eye-watering savagery. This little book tells the story of the magnificent wilderness that was once the domain of the buffalo, the prairie dog (little ratty things) and the Native American, and how the Wild West helped set the stage for America to become the most powerful country in the world and the proud home of the Big Mac and Mickey Mouse.

The ORIGINAL 13 STATES OF AMERICA

Chapter 2

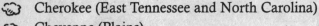 *IN THE BEGINNING*

Although most of the rest of the world had kissed goodbye to the Stone Age some centuries earlier, the Native Americans were living what was basically a stone age life until 'discovered' by the white man in the 16th century. They knew how to use stone, wood, skin and bone for their weapons and household objects, but knew nothing about metal. The men (braves) knew how to get their women (squaws) to carry all the heavy loads, and even made little sledges out of sticks to be pulled by their tame dogs, but knew nothing of horses or carts (let alone wheels). They knew about fire to cook and keep themselves warm with, but knew nothing about fridges in which to keep their drinks cool*. They knew everything there was to know about the properties of plants and the movements of wild animals, but hadn't a clue about the habits of the strange-looking men from distant lands (I'm not sure I do either!).

As we know from the telly, the Native Americans were divided up into lots of different tribes: nice ones, nasty ones, clever ones, stupid ones, fat ones, thin ones, tall ones, short ones, smelly ones. Seriously though, here's a list of some of the major tribes and where they came from:

- Apache (South Plains, South-West, East)
- Cherokee (East Tennessee and North Carolina)
- Cheyenne (Plains)
- Chinook (North-West Pacific coast)

---

* Nor did anyone else at that time! *Ed*

- Iroquois (North-East)
- Mohawk (New York)
- Navajo (New Mexico, Arizona, Utah)
- Sioux (Plains)

But what was life like for your average male ~~Redskin~~ – whoops! – Native American? Here's a sort of daily routine for your average bloke, on a non-war day.

1. Sunrise! Time for our man – let's call him Running Bare* – to get up.

NOT INVENTED YET. ED.

2. First off, lift wigwam (tent) flap, and check what sort of day it is. Kick dog and then squaw and ask her (not very politely) to get breakfast ready (the squaw, not the dog). Running Bare *would* have gone out to check the domestic animals and hens and stuff, but he wouldn't have had any. The family had to be content with what he and his mates could hunt or trap.

* Shouldn't that be Running Bear? Ed

Useless Fact No. 942

If it was a war day, this time would be spent putting on his make-up – sorry, warpaint – and sharpening his arrows.

3. Have a smoke with the rest of the lads before going out to catch supper. Running Bare & Co. would be pretty skilled with their bows and arrows, spears and slings, and knew how to set traps, dam rivers and dig pits for big animals (and big enemies) to fall into. They would eat anything that moved: bear, deer, rabbit, beaver, wild turkey . . .

Useless Fact No. 944

Tobacco was unheard of in Europe until it was brought back from the Americas.

4. Back from hunting, the boys would spend a few hours in the back garden (all million miles of it) cultivating maize and various vegetables to eat or smoke.

NOT INVENTED YET . ED.

5. Spend evening sitting by the fire, eating, smoking, singing and dancing, while the women sat around making clothes, gossiping, and having children.

All in all it was a pretty idyllic life for Running Bare and his chums, who had one of the most beautiful, bountiful and . . . er, big countries in the world all to themselves. Until one day . . .

Chapter 3

HERE COME
THE SPANIARDS

One day, in 1492, an Italian sailor-cum-tourist-cum-explorer-cum-adventurer, Christopher Columbus, bumped into an island (now called San Salvador), just off the coast of what turned out to be Florida. Having set out from the Old World (i.e. Europe, etc.), Columbus was actually looking for a new route to Asia but instead discovered the New World (i.e. America) which turned out to be much more fun. He rushed back to tell his patrons King Ferdinand and Queen Isabella of Spain (and all his explorer mates) amazing yarns about the vast riches (gold, silver, pearls and oodles of slaves) which were simply lying around for the taking. His voyage was responsible for the beginning of the mass invasion of the American continent by the Spanish Conquistadors (conquerors). In other words, it was all his fault.

Conquistadors

To begin with, the Spanish invaders, led by Cortez, travelled south to Mexico and Peru and fell upon the fabulous Aztec, Mayan and Inca civilizations (read *Aztecs*, in this series – by me). When the poor South Native Americans (is that right?) first set eyes on the heavily armoured soldiers astride their heavily armoured horses, firing their guns, they thought each couple was one monstrous, roaring beast. Silly, but quite understandable – especially if you don't get out much. When the Spaniards had plundered just about everything that hadn't actually been nailed down, and subdued the poor natives into the bargain, they looked greedily northwards. Since the South was so rich, it stood to reason that it would be the same further up country.

Tall Stories

The conquered Mexican Indians had a right laugh, telling the invaders amazing stories about treasures almost beyond the imagination. Stories like that of a huge tribe of Florida Indians that ran around in massive helmets of pure gold (and not much else), whose leader had been smothered in grease, then stretched into giantdom by his faithful (if somewhat over-keen) subjects. Stories about diamond-covered mountains that glistened like sugar-frosted fairy cakes. Stories about seven magical cities built out of just about everything you could imagine that was precious, inhabited by people who liked to sprinkle themselves with gold dust before going out to the shops. The Spaniards heard of strange tribes, some of whom sheltered under the shade of their enormous ears*, others who lived, for some obscure reason,

WHO ARE YOU CALLING BIG EARS?

* At least they'd have heard them coming. Ed
Very funny – I'll do the jokes, thank you. JF

under water, and an entire race of completely bald men in California whose queen had the biggest feet in the world.

Unfortunately, these tales were top-of-the-range porkies, probably designed by the fed-up natives to get rid of their oppressors as quickly as poss. As it turned out, the poor (well not *that* poor) Spanish soldiers, having trekked all the way into the main bit of America, found nothing but a few of the Mexican Indians' scruffy rellies who, like their southern brothers, had never seen a horse or a buffalo before, let alone swords, guns, or flash made-to-measure armour.

Useless Fact No. 946
The Conquistadors brought five mares and eleven stallions with them in 1519. Cortez's chum, Bernal Diaz, was heard to remark: 'After God, we owed the victory *[over Mexico]* to the horses.'

Useless Fact No. 947
Before the Spanish arrived with their horses, the horse had been extinct on the American continent for 10,000 years.

Chapter 4

HERE COMES EVERYBODY ELSE!

Pirates Ahoy

Despite all the Spaniards' power and influence, once the word got out about America and its treasures, they couldn't keep the rest of Europe at bay. English, French and Dutch pirates soon turned up like wasps round a jam sandwich, hanging around the coast in shoals,* picking off the Spanish treasure ships as they tried to get their precious pilfered plunder back home.

European Take-over

Eventually the 17th century saw the colonization of large bits of America by Europeans. The English built settlements all the way along the Atlantic Coast (the one facing England). They ended up spending most of their time fighting off the French, who'd already snapped up Louisiana (in the centre) and were having a go at California (in the west), which was then a part of Mexico.

Lizzie Beats 'em Soundly

The defeat of the Spanish Armada in 1588 by our own Elizabeth I's weedy little fleet really took the wind out of the Spaniards' sails. Their conquest of America was beginning to

* Shoals of wasps? *Ed*

lose its momentum,* especially as they continued to have no luck in finding gold and precious things in the middle bit. In addition, the natives were becoming restless and in 1680 an army of Pueblo Indians drove the Spanish settlers out of their capital, Santa Fe, killing over 400 and, much more to the point, capturing their vast herds of horses, which hitherto they'd not even been allowed to stroke. It was from these 400 horses that all those horses used by the 'Injuns' in the movies came.

Christianity? No Thanks!

As well as introducing horses, the Spaniards forced Christianity on the natives of America. As soon as they got the chance, the Pueblo Indians washed all that nasty 'Christianness' off with the juice of the Yucca (a sort of cactusy thing), becoming proper heathens again. They then forbade the use of any religious objects (crosses and stuff) and even the use of the Spanish language.

Fur Deal

Up in the north-east, right the way up into Canada, the French were searching for legendary gold and precious stones, but they found nothing. What they did manage to find was fur. Fur, fur and more fur, from the backs of all the poor beasts that got in their way – or rather the Indians' way. Needless to say, it was the Indians that put in the hard work, trapping, catching and skinning the animals.

* A bit like this. When do we get on to the Wild West? Ed
I'm just setting the scene. Be patient. JF

In return for the furs, the French gave the Indians iron, axes, knives, blankets, glass beads and of course – little mirrors (the Native Americans were as vain as the Native French).

Useless Fact No. 949

During the next couple of centuries horses (especially Spanish horses) became more valuable than practically anything else. The whole colonization of the West simply could not have happened without the Spanish horse: the country was just too big.

Fur Frenzy

In the end, the French got almost as much cash from trading fur as they would have done from the gold they were after in the first place. This was the beginning of the great American fur trade. Europe was well into a massive fashion craze for all things furry, and this new source was dead timely, as the European hunters had defrocked practically every fluffy creature that moved in their own vast forests.

Useless Fact No. 950

The French traders also promised to help the Native Indians (especially the Sioux, Hurons and Algonquins) fight the beastly Iroquois, using guns – which naturally scared the feathers right off 'em. The Hurons, by the way, had a nasty habit of capturing the Iroquois and eating them, which the Iroquois found rather annoying, to say the least.

VERY NICE, BUT I PREFER APACHES

Everywhere the French stopped, as they traded across America, they cheekily ran up the French flag and claimed the land as their own. By taking control of the Mississippi valley, which ran bang down the middle of the country, they reckoned they'd have a stranglehold on the whole continent. It would keep the English behind the Appalachian Mountains to the East and split the Spanish who occupied Florida and the South-West.

This bigger plan wasn't to be, but they did manage to colonize a *huge* chunk in the middle of America and call it Louisiana (today's Louisiana is a much shrunken state). Here they founded the city of New Orleans (they had their own *old* Orléans back home*) at the mouth of the Mississippi River right down in what we now call the deep South.

'Louisiana' Changes Hands

The vast lands of Louisiana, west of the Mississippi, were taken back off the French by the Spanish in 1762. The Spanish were forced to hand Louisiana back to the French again in 1800 but in 1803 the French cashed in their chips completely and flogged Louisiana to the newly formed United States of America, under Thomas Jefferson – 27 million dollars the lot (five cents an acre) – not bad, eh! It turned out that French boss Napoleon was a little strapped for the old readies and needed a fat wad of francs to rebuild his armies, who were beginning to get the worst of it in Europe. He didn't give a fig about America – he had far more worrying things to worry about back home.

* You don't say. *Ed*

Chapter 5

WHAT TO DO
WITH THE
🌀⇻ INDIANS?

Before the Wars of Independence, which resulted in the 1776 formation of the United States of America, relations between the British and the five 'civilized' Native American tribes from the South-East – the Cherokees, Choctaws, Creeks, Chickasaws and Seminoles – were really quite good. The Indians rather liked the British style and began to copy the white man's clothes, housing and even farming methods (they didn't go quite as far as taking tea in the afternoon, but you get the picture). They bought cattle and ploughs, and even grew cotton to weave into cloth. OK, they still fought and tortured each other in monstrous ways, like cutting off noses and ears and scalps, setting fire to each other's huts and killing men, women and children, but all that was part and parcel of being a fully paid-up 'Injun'. It couldn't be all work and *no* play.

Useless Fact No. 952
To scalp: the rather unpleasant custom of removing the scalp hair, with skin attached, of one's victim.

During the War of Independence, however, most of the forest Indians had taken up arms against the thirteen colonies (i.e. the United States) which meant that when the war ended they

SCALP-
FREE
ZONE

found themselves on the losing side – not that they actually gave a stuff about some rotten old treaty (the Treaty of Paris). But it all became a terrible headache for the new government. Settlers were continuing to pour across the Appalachian Mountains, providing entertainment for the Indians who were picking them off at will.

Bribes for All

The government acted quickly, dazzling them with blankets, food, jewellery (beads and stuff) and, more to the point, hard cash, in return for getting out of the forests and becoming nice well-behaved farmers on the western plains – which they did. Now, as you can imagine, this was all nonsense. You can't turn a tribal hunter-gatherer into a farmer overnight. The bigger tribes soon saw that this was the thin end of a very large wedge and one of the great Indian leaders, Tecumseh (a Shawnee), tried to get all the forest tribes together for a powwow (meeting) to try to get the support of the British in Canada. 'How can you sell a country?' he cried. 'You might just as well try to sell the air, the clouds and the sea.'

Unfortunately for the Indians, this didn't work and his warriors were defeated by the Americans in 1811 at Tippecanoe. Two years later the Shawnees' great leader was himself killed in battle and the rest of his tribe were pushed off to an Indian Territory on some rather awful land west of the Mississippi. Between 1820 and 1840, this land became a dumping ground for over 100,000 unwanted Redskins.

Chapter 6

WESTWARD HO?

The Great Move West

In the early part of the 19th century, there was a massive move west towards Oregon and California. Some, like the Mormons, went for religious reasons. All the Mormons wanted was to be left alone to live in their own way (lots of wives, etc.). They settled in Utah – Salt Lake City to be precise – and are still there to this day. But most of the pioneers packed up their homes because they'd heard scrummy stories about wide fertile plains that were ridiculously cheap to buy ($1.25 dollars per acre in 1800), and about a ready market for the grain that, once planted, practically leapt from the ground. The government were right behind the move as they saw it as a way of nabbing the land off the French and the Spanish.

Sea or Land?

There were two ways of getting to the west from the east. One was to go to New York and then travel south by sea, all the way round via the Gulf of Mexico and Cape Horn in South America – but this was expensive and dangerous. The other way was to travel west overland via the Oregon Trail. This also involved heavy risks and big questions, like . . . How far did they have to travel? How long would it take? Who would lead? How unpleasant *were* the natives? How much food and equipment would need to be taken? When would Disneyland be opening? And these were just the obvious ones.

Overnight Stay Only

The wagon trains rolled along the Oregon Trail from 1839, relatively peacefully apart from the ever-present risk of disease and the obvious hardship of being miles from the shops. Despite what you see in the movies, the Indians never actually attacked the brave travellers, as long as they stuck to the trail as they passed through the Indians' land. OK, they were often seen watching along the mountain ridges, waving their spears

HOW NICE!
THEY'RE WAVING

and everything,* but they only attacked when the settlers tried to take their land off them. (The American government often removed the Indians from an area, before surveying it and flogging it to eager settlers.) After all, pondered the Indians, what was the point of galloping round wagon trains making all that din (whooping and stuff), setting yourself up as a fairground shooting gallery for the well-armed settlers, who'd just hide behind their wagons and shoot you at will? Quite unnecessary, I expect they thought!

Useless Fact No. 955
The coloured or 'painted' horse (skewbald or piebald) was a favourite with the Indians because of its natural camouflage.

Mobile Homes
Life was very hard on the 'trains' of wagons that travelled hundreds of miles across the wide prairies and inhospitable deserts. It's interesting to note that the covered wagons were rarely pulled by horses, despite what all those old pioneer films would have us believe. Horses just weren't strong enough to pull them over the mountain ranges. After all, they were usually carrying a good six months' supplies, along with all the tools that would be necessary on arrival (weighing anything up to a ton). Mostly they used mules, or even more mostly, oxen, which were very cheap (a third of the price of mules), very slow (eight miles a day) and very, very stupid.

The families that did ignore the 'no horse' advice often had to abandon their wagons in the mountains and do the last bit on their backs (the horses' backs, that is). By the mid 1850s the trails, especially across the deserts, were littered with animal

* Everything? Ed

skeletons, broken wagons and even the remains of humans –
who were often left where they fell, with simple little crosses
made of sticks laid on their chests (or on their backs, if they fell
on their fronts*).

Togetherness
Later on, when the wagons reached the Missouri River on the
edge of the great wilderness, they'd rest at the little town of
Independence and join together to form long wagon trains,
seldom less than twenty in a line. The settlers would then
organize themselves in an almost military manner with a hired
captain, several lieutenants and even a quartermaster to ration
the food. Often the captains proved useless at the highly
responsible job of leading such a large operation and it was not
uncommon for there to be several change-overs before reach-
ing their destination.

The major problem was holding the train together, as some
wagons were much faster than others. The cattle, an essential
part of the entourage, couldn't be hurried and sometimes

* Thank you, Mr Farman, I think we might *just* have worked that out. Ed.

dropped behind. Often an overloaded wagon broke down or turned over and had to be repaired there and then. All in all, however, a great sense of community was forged, and every evening the wagons were drawn round in a circle, and within this space meals were cooked, meetings held, games organized for the kids and rather tedious mouth organ music was played long into the night.

Oregon or California?

By 1860, 175,000 honest if somewhat exhausted settlers had crossed the mighty plains and lofty mountains from the Mississippi to the promised land of California, while thousands more chose Oregon further north. As I said before, the more Americans that settled in California the more chance there was of eventually wresting it off the Mexicans – and it was the same story in Oregon with the British.

In 1846 the British Government put up their hands and gave up all claims to any Oregon land south of latitude 49 degrees North. As for California, the massive amount of settlers gradually brought America and Mexico to the brink of war – and indeed in 1846 war broke out. But it was a short-lived, one-sided battle – a David and Goliath tussle with Goliath (America) winning hands down (soon to become a habit). By 1847 Mexico had given up all her lands north of the Rio Grande and Gila Rivers to her big brother for a paltry 15 million dollars (the price of a big house in Hollywood today).

☞ Chapter 7

☞ GOLD!

In 1848 something happened that was to mightily speed up the colonizing of the West. James Marshall, an employee of John Sutter, a Sante Fe trader and all-round wheeler-dealer, found little bits of what turned out to be pure gold in the stream beside the sawmill which they were building on the fork of American River in the Sacramento Valley, California. Big Boss Sutter had created a little empire on an enormous tract of land he'd bought at a knockdown price off some Russian settlers who'd been ordered home by their boss, the Tsar. Sutter employed scores of migrant Morons* and hundreds of Indians who regarded him as a sort of king. Sutter called his little empire New Helvetia.

Keeping Secrets

Sutter, Marshall and the few Mormons who'd heard what was going on, kept the find a secret, as Sutter fully realized what a gold rush would do to his cushy little set-up. But other workers weren't daft and it soon dawned on them that by popping out in their tea break and scratching away at the little veins of gold that they found in the rocks, they could earn a month's pay in five minutes. In two months practically all Sutter's Mormon employees were dashing out after work and at weekends to scrabble for the precious specks. Before long Sutter found that he had no employees left – as, after a while, they didn't even bother to turn up. On 8 May 1848, a bag of gold

* I think you mean Mormons. Ed

dust from New Helvetia found its way to San Francisco, California, and before you could sneeze, news of the find was winging its way round the world . . .

The Great American Gold Rush had begun.

Gold Fever

It started with a mere handful of eager opportunists but, before you could say 'American Fork', the trickle had turned into a rushing river of gold-greedy prospectors. In a fascinating report in Dee Brown's book *The Westerners*, the author calls the migration the greatest movement of human beings, from every corner of the earth, since the Crusades. As for America itself, people throughout the land stopped what they were doing (in the middle of doing it) and packed up their belongings as best they could before heading off to California. In California itself, 40 per cent of all army regiments deserted their posts, and throughout the northern part of the state, town after town was emptied of all its menfolk.

California or Bust

As ever, California proved hard to reach. Most people travelled overland, but thousands of easterners leapt onto ships bound for California via Cape Horn. This was hazardous and expensive ($300, a small fortune) and extremely slow (eight months minimum) – and all this was the result of ludicrous newspaper articles claiming that the gold was inexhaustible.

Others went by sea to Panama, took the 'short cut' across the Isthmus of Panama to the Pacific and then waited for a proper ship to take them up to San Francisco. Fine in theory, but the Isthmus (try saying that while chewing a toffee) was jolly nasty – full of jungles, swamps and diseases and bitey things that killed you as soon as looked at you. Not only that but at Panama City there were thousands of men sleeping on the beaches waiting for the handful of ships that sailed back and forth up the coast. Nevertheless, 80,000 bright-eyed, bushy-tailed gold prospectors somehow arrived in California in the summer of 1849.

Travelling Light

But just as the early settlers had found before, the endless trail was hard and these prospector chappies were far from prepared. Some crazy young men even set out on horseback with no provisions whatsoever (not even a toothbrush). All along the trail were articles that had been chucked overboard to reduce weight: stoves, gridirons, tools, anvils, ovens, barrels, bedding and even sacks of grain and foodstuffs. More sinister were the rotting carcasses of horses (dead) and mules (also dead), still in harness, and still attached to broken-down wagons. The Indians probably thought it was Christmas and must

have had a high old time just picking up the stuff abandoned on their lands.

Slim Pickings

It's sad to report that, when it came right down to the nitty-gritty, there was more gritty than nitty. In other words, the large quantities of Californian gold that they all went out to find, simply weren't there. True, a few of the early prospectors made modest fortunes, but overall it was calculated that if the amount of gold found was divided by the men digging for it (then divided by the long hours they spent), the average rewards would be less than a dollar a day – not even enough to feed the average digger (especially with the highly inflated food prices charged by opportunist traders). Having said that, gold towns like Denver and Virginia City sprang up wherever there were gold-crazed men to exploit.

Marshall and Sutter

And what of the chaps who inadvertently started the whole thing off? Poor James Marshall (the guy who discovered the gold in the first place) could only stand by as the excited prospectors invaded his 640-acre claim and even hired armed guards to keep Marshall away from his own land (cheeky or what?). He ended up poverty-stricken, but, as so often happens in real life, as soon as he was dead, he was recognized as the man who started the gold rush, and a national monument was created where he was buried.

As for Sutter, he watched, gobsmacked, as the prospectors trampled his land and ate all his animals. When he appealed to the authorities, they said that his claim to what had for so long been his own land was invalid, as all he had to prove it was an ancient Mexican grant. Sutter ended up bankrupt, like Marshall, living in a cheap hotel in Washington, where he died in 1880.

Chapter 8

HERE COME THE COWBOYS

In the middle of the States was a large area called the Great Plains. Hot enough to bake a lizard in the summer months and cold enough to freeze a brass monkey in the winter. Much of the land was what we'd call desert, as there were few trees and no water (let alone bars or cafés). There were, however, great herds of hardy buffalo and rangy longhorn cattle and, of course, the people who lived off them – the Native American Indians.

Useless Fact No. 957

In 1521, two years after the conquest of Mexico by Cortez, a Spanish ship sailed from the island of Hispaniola with a number of Andalusian (Spanish, to you) cattle. It was from this shipment that all the thousands of wild longhorn cattle (their horns often stretched up to two metres across*) of the American plains were descended. The mean, grumpy and extremely fast longhorns were eventually crossed with the hefty, white-faced, but rather kind British Herefords, who were far easier to control.

* Could that be why they were called longhorns? Ed.

In 1830, when the cattle industry began, there were over 100,000 animals in Texas alone, most of which ran wild after the Texas Revolution – when the Texans took what is now Texas from the Mexicans. The cattle were claimed by the winners, who chased the poor Mexican landowners off their own land. These Texans (the first real cowboys), many of British descent, drove vast herds down to New Orleans or across to California to sell 'em. The cowboys (the term was first used as an insult) were rough, tough and really had it in for the Indians or any Mexican that was still stupid enough to be hanging around.

The Cattle Trail

But it wasn't all plain sailing – or ranching. After the Civil War of 1862–65 (between the victorious northern Union states and the southern Confederate states), the defeated Texans, mostly demobbed and wounded Confederate soldiers, crawled home to find their ranches wrecked and their cattle having a great time running about all over the place. The whole cattle business had collapsed while they'd been away playing soldiers. Hundreds more cowboys were then drafted in to drive the cattle on the hard and dust-choking trail north, where there was a bad shortage of good beef, or to the north-east to Sedalia to meet the newly laid eastbound railway.

Driving the long trail north was a dangerous business as there were many bands of what became known as jayhawkers or redlegs, not to mention savage Indians – all of whom were ready to set on them, and steal their herds.

The Pony Express

The first mail service began on 13 April 1860, when 49 letters and three newspapers were carried 1,980 miles from St Joseph, Missouri to Sacramento, California. Horses and riders were changed every twelve miles at Pony Express stations. As a service, the Pony Express was soon replaced by the telegraph, but while it lasted, the riders were considered to be heroes, braving the dangers of the Wild West and the hostile Indians. However, only one rider was ever killed. And he tripped over his postbag.*

Useless Fact No. 959

Did you know that ring doughnuts were supposed to have been invented by the girls that used to wait for the heroic Pony Express riders to race through their towns? The idea was that the riders wouldn't need to stop, but could spear the doughnuts onto their fingers or guns.

* No he didn't. Ed

How to Be a Cowboy

These were the basic qualifications needed to become a cowboy.

1. The belief that a life of adventure and thrills was far more important than money. (Pay was never above $30 a month.)

2. Willingness to be dirty, itchy and downright smelly – there were no washing facilities and therefore no clean underwear available for months on end.

3. Cowboys would often be of Scottish (like the Lone McRanger) or Irish stock – and of the Protestant faith. Having said that, a quarter of the cowboy crews were black. The black cowboys were never allowed to share the bunkhouses or socialize with their white 'pardners', which seems most unfair, if you ask me.

4. They had to be hard workers and would be expected to be totally loyal to their bosses and fellow cowfolk.

5. Cowboys would usually treat their horses better than their women. A good horse was the most important part of their equipment, and, let's face it, they spent far more time with them.

6. A cowboy would seldom use his fists in a fight – not if he had a gun. Fist-fighting was for wimps and took too long.

7. Cowboys hated the settlers and called them 'sod-busters'. A good cowboy also loathed sheepmen – and the little bleaters they looked after. No self-respecting cowboy would ever eat mutton or lamb, or green vegetables, or come to that anything apart from beans and beef.

8. Cowboys' conversation was usually rude and crude and full of foul swearing (punctuated by spitting) – though it must be said, they were never known for talking that much anyway.

Cowboy Outfit

Totally practical, this is thought to have been copied from the
gauchos (cattle-herders) of South America:

- Hat: to keep sun and rain off face, to drink out of, and
  for arrows to go through.
- Bandana: to protect neck, to pull over mouth to stop
  dust.
- Leather chaps: to
  protect legs from cow
  horns and thorny
  bushes.
- Long leather boots:
  ditto, and good
  protection
  against snakes.
- Denim jeans:
  ditto.

TEN GALLON HAT

NECKERCHIEF

LEVI'S

LEATHER CHAPS

COWDOG

COWBOY BOOTS →

COWBOY KIT

Useless Fact No. 961

After it was all over and the Wild West was just a fantasy in the
minds of the eastern Americans, this cowboy costume became a
macho symbol . . . manly, brave, strong.

Useless Fact No. 962

Movie cowboys like Hopalong Cassidy and the Lone Ranger wore fringed, shiny costumes which were invented by Hollywood. The reality was that cowboys, more often than not, looked like down-and-out tramps.

Rail Fever

As the railroad stretched further and further into the interior, rough and ready cowtowns like Dodge City, Ellsworth and Wichita sprang up to break the journey and service the various needs of the cowboys or, in other words, relieve them of their hard-earned wages. These isolated settlements (known as one-horse towns) naturally attracted all the dregs of society – bank robbers, tricksters, gamblers, hired killers and even bank managers (urgh!).

Useless Fact No. 964

It was from this relatively short period in history (maybe as little as 40 years) that all the great stories of the 'Wild West' were born. Brave and legendary lawmen like Wyatt Earp and Wild Bill Hickok gained fame and fortune as they tried against all odds to keep some kind of order.

More Settlers

This all went brilliantly for the rich cattlemen until around 1885, when there were simply too many animals for the over-nibbled prairies. Then, lo and behold, the weather turned 'real mean': scorching summers with no rain, followed by freezing snow-laden winters. So bad that the poor weakened beasts found it difficult to survive. So bad, in fact, that half of them didn't. Just to make things worse, the new homesteaders decided to fence in their land with the newly invented barbed wire (Joseph Glidden, 1874) to keep the starving cattle out. The ensuing fights became so serious (the cattlemen had a nasty habit of hanging the homesteaders if they could find a suitable tree), that troops had to be brought in. For all these reasons, the last great cattle drives were over by 1895.

Beef Bonanza

The big money was now in massive cattle ranches and between 1870 and 1890, 37 ranches worth nigh on $34,000,000 spread all the way across Nebraska, Kansas, Montana, Wyoming and Colorado. On this territory, wells were dug and hay was grown for cow food, and the cowboy's life became one of fencing, digging ditches, mowing and stacking hay, watering, feeding, and branding, which, as you can imagine, they found really boring and not a bit what a proper cowboy had been led to expect. As they sat in their cosy bunkhouses the cowboys dreamed wistfully of the great drives north, sitting round the campfires, singing songs and eating beans, beans and more beans – and farting the night away to their hearts' content.*

* Please, do we really need to know this? Ed

By the 1890s, however, many of the big beef players went bankrupt, as America reeled from the competition from Argentinian and Australian cattle. Beef sales to Europe, for instance, plummeted by 50%, and by the turn of the century, the western cattle boom was well and truly over.

Chapter 9

THE MORE
THE MERRIER

As the stream of wagons trundled laboriously across the wide inhospitable plains of the wild and woolly west, it occurred to some that despite the dry climate, it might be possible to run a homestead bang in the middle. This had the added advantage of cutting the blinking journey in half. After the Civil War of 1862–65 (between the northern Union states and the southern Confederate states*), thousands, including many from far

COULD YOU POP
NEXT DOOR FOR
SOME SUGAR

* You've already said that once. Ed

distant shores, decided to follow suit and the cultivation and colonization of the Great Plains began in earnest.

Why? Simple! The land was dirt cheap and the amount you could have was limited only by the amount you reckoned you could cultivate. The railway companies, who, having got in there first, owned massive chunks of prairie, were also flogging it off to finance the ever-growing railroad. Also, as far away as Scandinavia and Europe, advertisements told stories of a promised land, full of milk and honey, where practically anything would grow (cows and bees, for instance?). These glossy ads particularly appealed to farmers living in cold, damp, unforgiving climates.

Cheap Land Alert

In 1862, the controversial Homestead Act made land the ultimate in real cheap. Settlers were allowed to farm 160 acres (65 hectares) for absolutely nothing provided they stuck it out for five years, after which it became legally theirs. The problem was that all the good fertile land went immediately to the railroad companies or the government, or even to dodgy but smart landgrabbers, leaving the second-rate areas to the rest. The other problem was that 160 acres wasn't enough (believe it or not) to sustain a family in such a harsh country, so in 1873 the government offered them the same amount again, provided they planted at least one acre (0.4 hectare) of trees (for the Indians to hide behind?).

Useless Fact No. 966

The thing about America is that it's a bit like an inside-out sandwich: all the nice bits on the outside (the coastal areas) and the dry boring old crusty bit on the inside (the Great Plains).

Somewhere to Live

So there they were, Mr and Mrs Jørgensson and all the little Jørgenssons, fresh off the boat from Sweden, standing in the middle of nowhere, with no sign of life as far as they could see. What to do first? Build some kind of shelter, perhaps? But what with? There were no trees (yet), therefore no wood. No bricks, no cement, no wallpaper and no DIY stores just round the corner. Blimey, there weren't even any corners for the DIY stores to be around.

Some Way to Build

Many early settlers, instead of building up (on account of having nothing to build up *with*), cut their losses and built down and across. In other words, they dug primitive shelters into the hillsides or banks. Fine in theory, if you didn't mind lumps of dirt or the odd cow falling through your roof.

Others cut blocks of turf (sods to you*) and laid them like bricks, building rather snazzy if somewhat simple (no Jacuzzis

* Sods to you too! Ed
Sods was and is the proper name for blocks of turf. JF

or billiard rooms) little houses, which they plastered inside and out with a mixture of sand and clay. All very well, till the deluges of rain came to soak them through and through and even wash some away completely.

Something to Heat

And how did they heat their homes or even cook meals with no wood, coal, electricity or North Sea Oil? The answer, I'm afraid to say, stood outside, mooing in the yard. No, they didn't set fire to their cows – they burned what the cows produced . . . dung, which, I'm also afraid to say, sometimes gave rather an unpleasant tang to Mum's already less than subtle cuisine.

Something to Eat

Building houses and cultivating plains tends to make one hungry. Normally Mum would have nipped down to the local grocer and bought some supplies. But there was nothing to buy and nowhere to buy it, so the new settlers had to rely on what they had brought with them until what they were attempting to grow grew (if you see what I mean).

Weather Report

It was then that it began to dawn on the settlers that all those glowing reports in the ads back home had been a touch fanciful to say the least. They hadn't informed them that the summers would often reach temperatures of over 38°C (100°F), baking the land harder than Mum's bread. And they hadn't mentioned the constant howling winds that could drive a sane man mad. And what about those summer winds that would pass over the land like industrial blowheaters, withering and singeing the brand new cornfields? Or the freezing winter gales which would ram snow through every tiny crack in the poorly built houses and chill the poor newcomers to the very marrow?

But then that's advertising for you.

Often the horse- or ox-drawn ploughs would simply refuse to even consider breaking up the top soil; and there'd be hardly enough water to keep the family alive, let alone water the shrivelling crops. And then there wouldn't be enough wood to make a chair, let alone put up fences to keep the cattle from strolling off into the wilderness. I suppose that was why they were made to grow trees.

Then, in the 1870s, to cap it all, just as everyone was beginning to cope with the ridiculously extreme conditions, along came plagues of grasshoppers, who cheerfully stopped for lunch (uninvited) and ate everything in sight. They hadn't mentioned *them* in the ads either. At this point, many of the new farmers simply threw up their blistered hands, admitted defeat and returned home, broke and disillusioned.

Here Come the Trains

The answer to all the hardships and deprivations came, oddly enough, with the railways, which brought food, clothing and, thank God, timber for barns, fences and furniture for the home – and even for the home itself. Equally important were the newly developed seeds and specially invented tools and farm implements, like the steel plough that went through the soil like a hot knife through butter. In fact, all the stuff necessary to run an efficient farm (provided they could borrow the dollars to pay for it). Best of all, thanks to clever Brits like James Watt and Thomas Newcomen, along came steam-powered agricultural machines which increased the area a man could cultivate well over ten times. Between 1866 and 1898 the output of wheat, which had a ready market in Europe and the

← FIRST TRAIN SPOTTERS

---

* What's a bushel, eh? Ed
A measure of capacity equal to 8 gallons (36.4 litres). JF

east, rose from 152 million bushels* to 675 million. And it was here that the railways really came into their own – as a means of getting the grain to the coast, from where it would be shipped to the marketplaces of the world.

Western Women

So far we've talked mostly about men and what they did in the West, but the women played an equal part in the drama. Most women had to do their share of the gruelling farm work, before getting down to more traditionally womanly functions like feeding the family, washing, making and mending their clothes, and tending and teaching the nippers (not to mention actually having them).

We'll meet a couple of famous Western Women in the next chapter.

Chapter 10

THE BAD BOYS (AND GIRLS) OF THE WILD WEST

The new money flooding into the West attracted another sort of pioneer – the devil-may-care law-breaker. Every sort of cheat, murderer, liar, robber, card-sharp, double-glazing salesman and professional hit-person found their way into the frontier towns. In the beginning most of these towns were pretty short on law and order (like *none*!).

Here are just a few of the best (or worst) characters . . .

William Quantrill

Known as 'The Bloodiest Man in American History', our Will, with his band of merry men, hit town after town, looting, burning, killing and parking their horses where they shouldn't.

His most famous raid was on Lawrence, Kansas, in 1863, where (and when) he and his men managed to massacre 200 honest citizens and injure a further 600. All this before his death, aged only 27 years.

Jesse James

Jesse James did his apprenticeship with the Quantrill gang before forming his own family business, with his relatives – the Youngers. He and his gang earned fame and fortune terrorizing the border state of Missouri. Eventually the gang were killed, but Jesse escaped with a reward of $10,000 on his head (under his hat, no doubt). He was eventually shot in the back, aged 34, by his best friend Bob Ford in 1882, while straightening a picture in his own house. With best friends like that who needs enemies (or pictures)?*

Useless Fact No. 969
Bob Ford was taken out by a shotgun blast from Ed Kelly, another notorious relly of the Youngers, in 1892.

Tiburcio Vasquez

A murderer from the tender age of 17 (bless 'im), Vasquez saw himself as a kind of Mexican Robin Hood, taking it out on the white Californian settlers, male and female, who he reckoned had stolen his homeland from his people. Vasquez robbed and killed across the state until hanged in 1875 – when, not surprisingly, he stopped.

John Wesley Hardin

Gambler and murderer from 15 years old, Hardin studied the law whilst in prison – which was a bit late, when you think

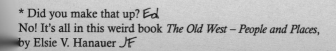
* Did you make that up? Ed
No! It's all in this weird book *The Old West – People and Places*, by Elsie V. Hanauer JF

about it. When released aged 41, Hardin practised as a lawyer, but the lure of quick money at the gambling tables drew him back to his old haunts (and his old mates, who still haunted the haunts). In 1895, during a minor argument over a hand of cards in an El Paso saloon, he was shot in the back of the head by the irate loser.

Clay Allison

A famous cowboy turned gunfighter who only killed people who, in his humble opinion, deserved it, Clay Allison was a kind of unofficial sheriff-cum-executioner. One of the fastest draws in the West, Allison was finally killed in 1887 when he carelessly tumbled out of his wagon (probably drunk), which promptly ran over his neck.

Black Bart

Properly known as Charles Bolton, Black Bart was famous for being the only man to hold up stagecoaches without either being on a horse (he was scared of 'em) or with a gun (he hated loud bangs).* Bolton was a wealthy mine-owner, but for seven years, every single time he left San Francisco to visit one of the mines, it was noticed that a Wells Fargo mail coach managed to get itself robbed. He was finally caught red-handed and sent to prison, where he was as good as the gold in his mines. As a result, Black Bart was released after only six years and lived happily ever after.

Billy the Kid

King of the bandits, Billy the Kid (William Bonney in real life) first managed to kill someone at 12 and thought it best to leave home (parents get so funny about that sort of thing). Slightly weak in the old head department, Billy the half-(or maybe quarter-)wit began a fascinating career as a gunslinger and robber until, at the ripe old age of 21, after killing 21 men (coincidence or what?), he was shot by the famous lawman, Pat Garrett.

Frank Leslie

Leslie never really travelled far from Arizona, where he built one of the *best* reputations as their *worst* killer. He came to the rough, tough town of Tombstone hoping to find gold, but found bars and women instead. While working as a barman in the Oriental Saloon, he shot ten men in one go, and then a little later, his wife. (If he used a pair of six-shooters, by my calculation, he must have had a bullet left . . .) The law didn't seem to mind the former, but he got 25 years for killing the missus.

* How did he do it then? Ed
Maybe he used a pea-shooter. JF

Kate Elder

Six foot tall (nearly two metres), with a face that they said would turn milk sour, Kate, strangely, had no trouble attracting the opposite sex. The most famous 'lady of the night' in the West, she started up in Dodge City, but after a brief affair with Doc Holliday (Marshall Wyatt Earp's famous sidekick) she established a notorious brothel in Kansas City which she ran very successfully until her death in 1889.

FASTEST DRAWERS IN THE WEST

The Apache Kid

The Apache Kid (as he was nicknamed) was a highly respected sergeant with the Apache Scouts (sneaky Indians who helped the cavalry seek out enemy tribes). As a matter of honour he was compelled to murder the man who he reckoned killed his dad, but the pesky paleface law didn't allow that sort of thing and he was arrested. The Apache Kid, who couldn't see what he'd done wrong, promptly put paid to his two guards and began the worst one-man terror campaign that Arizona had ever seen – murdering and robbing at will. Despite a $5,000 reward for his capture – dead or alive – the kid was never caught.

George Parrott

Alias Big Nose George, he was more famous for his horrible fate than for his life as a cattle rustler and killer. While trying to escape, George was caught and hung by a bunch of rather cross citizens in 1880. A young doctor was given the body to play with – sorry, *dissect* for medical research – but he got a bit carried away. Firstly, he cut the top off old George's skull and kept it as a rather macabre ornament, then he skinned the body and made himself a nice pair of shoes and a flash pocket-book to match. Beats pigskin, I suppose.

Useless Fact No. 971

For over 75 years nobody could remember what happened to the rest of poor George, until someone discovered an old, extremely smelly barrel, with our skinless hero neatly arranged inside. Urghh!

Cherokee Bill

Crawford Goldsby, otherwise known as Cherokee Bill, shot his first victim at 18 and then joined the famous Cook gang in Oklahoma. In two years he personally gunned down thirteen men, obviously an unlucky number because he was eventually captured and hanged in front of his proud mum and a hundred other fans in 1896.

Pearl Hart

Pearl achieved fame not only for being the last person to rob a stagecoach but also for being a woman in a man's job. She and her male partner got away with $400 but were caught almost immediately by the chasing posse. Pearl was sentenced to five years in Yuma Prison, but it turned out they had nowhere to put women at Yuma so they let her out on parole. For years afterwards she earned a sort of living as a notorious sideshow personality, billed as Arizona's Only Lady Bandit.

Joaquim Murieta

Another Mexican with a grudge against the white Americans in California. Understandable really, since a bunch of drunken miners had hanged his brother and raped his wife. Joaquim had come from Soñora, Mexico, to search for gold but when all this nastiness happened he decided to spend his life *robbing* gold instead of digging for it. A Texas Ranger (a sort of cowboy policeman) finally caught up with him and after a bit of severe to-ing and fro-ing returned to California with just his head in his saddlebag in order to claim the $1,000 reward.

₰ Chapter 11

₰ TAMING THE INDIANS

It's funny, but up until the 1860s, the rest of America just hadn't given a darn about the Great Plains of North America. To them, it was just a boring old desert only really fit for savages. On the other hand, the Indians (Native Americans) who lived there had always felt a trifle niggled by all those paleface pioneers and greedy gold-miners who, for years, had trekked willy-nilly across their homeland on their way to the West and the mountains, nicking and gnawing all their precious buffalo on the way. Fair do's, really! Imagine someone trampling across *your* back garden, leaving all their rubbish, digging all your vegetables and eating all your pets. I wonder what Neighbourhood Watch would have to say about that?

Carry On Pioneering?
But when some of these pioneers decided not to bother plodding on to the distant West and simply plonked themselves down in the middle of what the Indians regarded as *their* land, it was the last straw (or should I say feather?). And if that wasn't bad enough, the poor old Indians were then forced to sign treaties promising: a) not to harm the blinking settlers and b) to give up bits of their sacred hunting ground to them – flipping cheek!

Then – can you believe it? – on top of all that, the Indians had to endure those great iron monsters trundling across their

56

sacred lands, belching steam and frightening their buffalo half out of their skins. The Cheyenne top man, Chief Roman Nose (odd name!*), had this to say on the subject:

> *We will not have the wagons which make a noise*
> [steam engines] *in the hunting grounds of the buffalo.*
> *If the palefaces come further into our land,*
> *there will be the scalps of your brethren*
> *in the wigwams of the Cheyennes.*
> *I have spoken.*

I bet those palefaces might just have got the point!

Buffalo to Go
Between 1840 and 1890 the buffalo herds shrank from 40,000,000 to a mere and unbelievable 1,000 animals. Most of them had been killed first by the railway construction crews and miners for food, then by wealthy Europeans purely for fun and then by greedy hunters for their valuable skins.

Useless Fact No. 973
William Cody, the famous and heroic (to some people) 'Buffalo Bill', killed 4,280 of the poor buffalo in a year, thus contributing to the worst animal slaughter the world has ever seen before or since.

In the end the buffalo were declared off-limits to the Indians (can you imagine?) – which made them madder than ever – and across the West there was a feverish competition among the whites to find and destroy the very last herd on the plains and, better still, the very last animal. The net result of all this

* It probably loses something in translation. JF

was that by the late 1880s there were just 26 buffalo left in Wyoming, ten in Montana and a pitiful and lonely four in the whole of Dakota. I wonder what today's conservationists would make of that?

Useless Fact No. 974

The buffalo weren't really buffalo – they were bison (*Bison americanus*). These massive animals (nearly two metres high at the shoulder) are now extinct in the wild.

I THINK THEY'RE TRYING TO TELL US SOMETHIN'

Indian Wars

But it wasn't just the buffalo who were endangered. The very lifeline of the Native American Indian was being stretched to the limit. They finally saw red* and began attacking the paleface camps and settlements in earnest. In 1864 a Colonel John Chivington took revenge and charged on two peaceful Cheyenne tribes. Of the 133 resident Indians he managed to slaughter 105 men, women and children. All the bodies, irrespective of size, were scalped (they were all at it in those

* I've warned you. Ed

days) and mutilated beyond recognition. And they called the *Indians* savages . . .

Red Cloud's War

The next big confrontation was won by the Indians who were fed up with the constant stream of miners on the Bozeman Trail. (This had barged through their happy hunting grounds on its way to the goldfields of Montana.) The Sioux (now armed with rifles), under Red Cloud, attacked the forts that the soldiers were trying to build to protect the travellers, and managed to kill 81 of 'em. It obviously put the wind up the government for eventually, in 1868, they agreed to close the Bozeman Trail and allow the Sioux to hang on to their lands, which was mighty big of them, don't you think?

Strong Reservations

Despite this victory, Red Cloud, realizing just how powerful the palefaces were becoming, was talked into settling on a reservation, where he and his people would be

given housing, food and clothing (new Indian outfits), and taught to farm. The trouble was that any proper, self-respecting Indian thought farming was

far too sissy and would have nothing to do with it. Consequently many refused to go to the reservation, and in 1874 a certain George Armstrong Custer (nicknamed Yellow Hair*) led a group of soldiers into the Black Hills of Dakota, which were still home to the Indians. These soldiers apparently stumbled on lots of what the Indians called 'yellow metal' and when they returned with the news, there was a new and massive gold rush to the mountains – despite them being on the lands given to the Sioux in the 1868 treaty.

As this went on, more and more Sioux refused to go to the reservation and many who'd gone earlier left to join up with the likes of Crazy Horse, Sitting Bull and the other big Indian chiefs. The army responded by *ordering* them all to go to the reservation by 31 January 1876 – or else! But by then Sitting Bull and Crazy Horse had had enough, and along with the might of the Cheyenne nation, got out their bows, arrows, spears, guns, tomahawks, scalping equipment, etc., and prepared for a massive showdown.

Custer's Last Stand

At this famous battle in 1876, Custer and his 225 men were cut to shreds during the Battle of the Little Bighorn by the largest bunch of Indians ever assembled. This sent the American people into a frenzy of rage, claiming that it was a massacre and demanding revenge against the Indians. Sitting Bull calmly stated that 'they came to kill us and got killed themselves.' Tough bananas,* I expect he thought.

Despite winning the battle, the Sioux lost the overall war and the tribe (Sitting Bull escaped, by the way) was escorted back to the reservation, their feathers between their legs. Once there, they all got ill with whooping cough (probably from too

* Why was that? Ed
Because he had *black* hair, stupid. JF
** He wouldn't have known what bananas were. Ed

much whooping!), but nevertheless believed that a new spiritual leader was on his way to come and save them (how many times have we all heard that?). This obsession made the downtrodden Indians strong again, dancing around, waving their tomahawks and making a dreadful din, calling for this Messiah to come pretty soonish. This, in turn, put the wind up their paleface neighbours, so much so that, before long, the army was called in. Every single Indian, whatever tribe he or she came from, was then ordered to live on designated reservations. Actually, they had no real choice, as the source of their staple food (the buffalo burger), had been all but wiped out.

Best Forget

At this point, most Americans put the old Indian problem onto the back burner and forgot all about those pesky primitives. After all, they thought, the savages had nice new reservations and were getting fed into the bargain – so what was the big deal? But in 1889 it all started to go wonky again. The Indians, as you might have guessed, turned out be useless at farming and, to make matters worse, kept catching weasels* – which had a habit of killing hundreds of their increasingly spotty kids. They just weren't used to living like this. Then their meat ration was chopped down the

* Don't you mean measles? Ed

middle and they rather inconsiderately (according to the authorities) began to starve.

More Dancing

But then, out of the blue, they all began to leap about in a very odd fashion and sing weird, squeaky, spooky songs in the middle of the night. These gatherings became known as the Ghost Dances which basically called on their spirits to get them out of the dreadful mess they'd gotten themselves into. The eerie sounds drifting across from the reservation freaked out the local homesteaders, who thought the rowdy redskins had either gone bonkers – or were preparing for another war . . .

Dead Bull

On 15 December 1893, Sitting Bull, boss man of the Sioux, was shot dead, having been accused (wrongly) of heading the Ghost Dances. This frightened the Sioux, who promptly ran away. But they were led back to a little settlement called Wounded Knee by soldiers and told to give up their old rusty weapons and be good Indians. To cut a medium story very short, a fight broke out and 84 men, 44 women and 18 children were all wounded in the knee* – sorry, massacred – as they tried to run away. For the Sioux, all their dreams of salvation were shattered. They promised to be good Indians and went meekly back to their reservations, bowed, broken, never to be a problem again.

Memories are Made of This

The golden days of the West were now but a memory. Nobody in America cared any more about the wide open plains (except

* Bad taste or what? Ed

p'raps the poor old Indians). All attention was now on the towns and factories of the east, and the new pioneers were whizzkid inventors, boring bankers and poncy insurance agents. Cattle barons and gold-miners were a thing of the past. But it was time for the memories to be enhanced, glamorized and made respectable so that nice Americans could lie in their beds with a clear conscience.

Here Comes Buffalo Bill

William Frederick Cody (see page 56), ex-Pony Express rider and buffalo hunter, headed the first spectacular Wild West Show (even though he'd never been a cowboy himself) in 1883. The shows, loved by people in America and all over the world, staged huge battles between the handsome cowboys and the villainous Indians, daring stagecoach hold-ups and brilliant

BIG 'EAD

exhibitions of riding, cattle-roping and sharp-shooting. The stars included the notorious Sitting Bull, and Annie Oakley, the girl cowboy. How tragic that even Sitting Bull, Chief of the Sioux, sold out and acted in a show that told such a false story.

Useless Fact No. 975
Cody, Wyoming, is where Buffalo Bill was born. It is named after him.

America had trashed one heritage and created another. These days the Wild West only exists in romanticized films and tacky Disneyland spectacles. The Indians are now reduced to living on garbage-strewn reservations and running gambling casinos. It's all such a terrible, terrible shame.

💨 TIME'S UP

So there you have it – the beginning, middle and end of perhaps the most violent and romantic period in American history, all for the price of a burger.* If you want to read more, and I really wouldn't blame you, saddle up your horse, and mosey on downtown to the library where some old (or young) critter might just help you find the section on American history, and all the really nasty and rude bits my editor made me leave out.

If you think you know enough, and I know exactly how you feel, then trot up Main Street, and hitch up to your local bookshop where you should be able to find some more in this fabulous series. Until then, pardners, keep your gun hand free, and, till the next time, *adios amigos*!

* I know which I'd prefer. Ed